SALSA

MY FAVORITE MUSIC

Sierra Wilson

AV2
www.openlightbox.com

AV2

Step 1
Go to **www.openlightbox.com**

Step 2
Enter this unique code
GXSLWFWT8

Step 3
Explore your interactive eBook!

Your interactive eBook comes with...

AV2 is optimized for use on any device

- **Audio** Listen to the entire book read aloud
- **Videos** Watch informative video clips
- **Weblinks** Gain additional information for research
- **Try This!** Complete activities and hands-on experiments
- **Key Words** Study vocabulary, and complete a matching word activity
- **Quizzes** Test your knowledge
- **Slideshows** View images and captions
- **Share** Share titles within your Learning Management System (LMS) or Library Circulation System
- **Citation** Create bibliographical references following APA, CMOS, and MLA styles

This title is part of our AV2 digital subscription

1-Year K–5 Subscription
ISBN 978-1-7911-3320-7

Access hundreds of AV2 titles with our digital subscription.
Sign up for a FREE trial at **www.openlightbox.com/trial**

The digital components of this book are guaranteed to stay active for at least five years from the date of publication.

SALSA

Contents

I love music.

Salsa is my favorite kind of music.

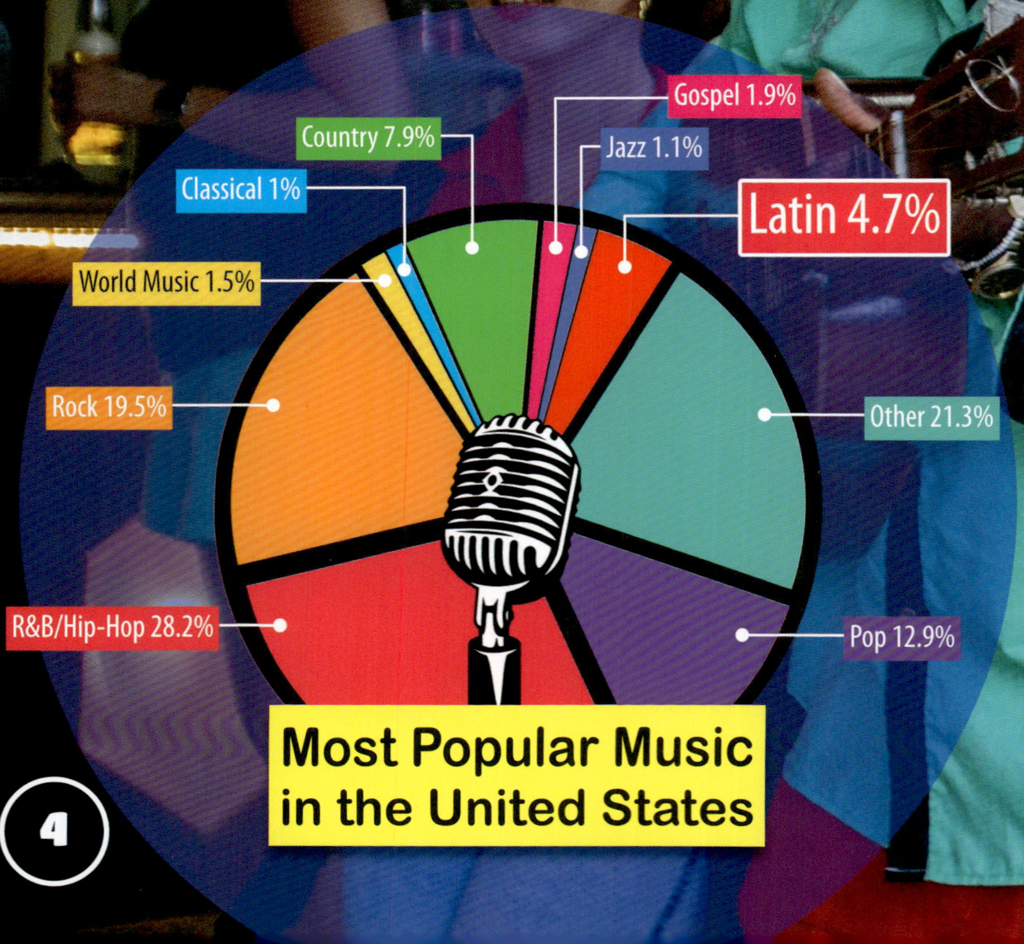

Most Popular Music in the United States

Salsa music began in New York City in the 1940s.

Salsa is made up of different musical styles.

Most salsa comes from mixing Cuban music with jazz music.

Many of the first salsa musicians came from places such as Puerto Rico and Cuba.

Salsa music was played to get people dancing.

Salsa singers add their own touches to the music.

They may invite other people to sing with them.

Many salsa songs talk about love and life.

Some are about problems people face.

Brass instruments such as trumpets and trombones give salsa its thrilling sound.

Congas, bongos, timbales, and other drums help keep the beat.

I like to play salsa music with my friends.

Each of us plays a different instrument.

Playing in a band teaches us how to work together.

Today, salsa is popular around the world.

Cali, a city in Colombia, is known as the "world capital of salsa."

Every year, people from all over the world come to its salsa festival.

I love salsa music.

It makes me want to dance!

SALSA FACTS

These pages provide detailed information that expands on the interesting facts found in the book. They are intended to be used by adults as a learning support to help young readers round out their knowledge of each musical genre featured in the *My Favorite Music* series.

Pages 4–5

I love music. Salsa is my favorite kind of music. Music is the name given to sounds made with voices or musical instruments and put together in a way that conveys emotion. People use music to express themselves. Salsa is one of the most popular forms of Latin music around the world. There are many types of salsa music. Among them are *salsa dura*, which is mainly instrumental, and *salsa romantica*, which has a soft, smooth sound. Salsa music is a genre that continues to evolve.

Pages 6–7

Salsa is made up of different musical styles. Many Latin immigrants came to New York City, bringing their musical traditions with them. Some formed bands and played Latin music such as mambo, bomba, and plena for local audiences. Radio stations and dance halls grew the popularity of Latin music. Musicians began experimenting and combining other musical styles, such as jazz, into their music. Soon, salsa was born.

Pages 8–9

Many of the first salsa musicians came from places such as Puerto Rico and Cuba. One of the most popular early salsa musicians was the famous Cuban-American singer Celia Cruz. She is known as the Queen of Salsa. Immigrants from Puerto Rico, such as Tito Rodríguez, were some of the other earliest salsa stars. These salsa musicians added ideas from their own cultures and musical backgrounds to continue evolving the sound of salsa. The goal of their music was to make people want to dance.

Pages 10–11

Salsa singers add their own touches to the music. Salsa music is typically sung in Spanish. While songs tend to have established lyrics, vocalists are encouraged to improvise while they sing. Not only does this help make the song their own, it also introduces an element of spontaneity to its sound. Many salsa songs are performed using the call-and-response technique. This is where the lead vocalist sings a line or section, and the choir or band sings another line or section in response.

Pages 12–13

Many salsa songs talk about love and life. Salsa lyrics are often about matters of the heart, Latin culture, or simply the joys of celebrating life. However, this type of music has also been used to draw attention to concerns the Latin community has had over the years. Salsa songs have been written to protest social issues, such as racism, and to highlight the difficulties immigrants can face in a new country.

Pages 14–15

Brass instruments such as trumpets and trombones give salsa its thrilling sound. Salsa bands can include a wide variety of instruments. Some of the most important are brass instruments. Trumpets, trombones, and saxophones help to create the melody and add a vibrancy to the music being performed. Percussion instruments produce the pulsating rhythm of salsa. A variety of drums, as well as claves, güiros, and cowbells, are used to set and layer the rhythm.

Pages 16–17

I like to play salsa music with my friends. Playing music with others helps teach children cooperation, teamwork, and how to achieve goals. Children who regularly play music tend to have more confidence and get along better with others. Some students learn better in groups because they do not feel the pressure of having to learn on their own.

Pages 18–19

Today, salsa is popular around the world. While New York City is known as the birthplace of salsa, Santiago de Cali has claimed the title of "world capital of salsa." The music has become a way of life in the city. Some of the world's top salsa dancers and musicians have hailed from Cali. The annual World Salsa Festival, which features performers and guests from around the world, is held there every year. Cali's residents have also created a unique style of salsa, called *salsa caleña*, or Colombian salsa. This style of salsa is now performed around the globe.

Pages 20–21

I love salsa music. Recent studies suggest that learning and practicing music can be beneficial to a child's ability to learn. Among these benefits are improved motor skills and dexterity, increased test scores, and even raised Intelligence Quotient, or IQ, scores. Learning music at an early age has also been shown to aid in language development and to improve reading and listening skills.

SIGHT WORDS

Research has shown that as much as 65 percent of all written material published in English is made up of 300 words. These 300 words cannot be taught using pictures or learned by sounding them out. They must be recognized by sight. This book contains 67 common sight words tc help young readers improve their reading fluency and comprehension. This book also teaches young readers several important content words. These words are paired with pictures to aid in learning and improve understanding.

Page	Sight Words First Appearance
4	country, I, in, is, kind, most, my, of, other, states, the, world
5	began, city, new
6	different, made, up
7	comes, from, with
9	and, as, came, first, get, many, people, places, such, to, was
10	add, own, their
11	may, them, they
13	about, are, face, life, some, songs, talk
14	give, its, sound
15	help, keep
16	a, each, like, play, us
17	how, together, work
18	around
19	all, every, over, year
21	it, makes, me, want

Page	Content Words First Appearance
4	classical, gospel, hip-hop, jazz, Latin, music, pop, R&B, rock, salsa, United States
5	New York City
6	styles
9	Cuba, musicians, Puerto Rico,
10	singers, touches
13	problems
14	instruments, trombones, trumpets
15	beat, bongos, congas, drums, timbales
16	friends
17	band
18	Cali, capital, Colombia
19	festival

Published by Lightbox Learning Inc.
276 5th Avenue, Suite 704 #917
New York, NY 10001
Website: www.openlightbox.com

Library of Congress Cataloging-in-Publication Data
Names: Wilson, Sierra, author.
Title: Salsa / Sierra Wilson.
Description: New York : Lightbox Learning Inc., 2025. | Series: My favorite music | Audience: Grades 2-3
Identifiers: LCCN 2024048584 (print) | LCCN 2024048585 (ebook) | ISBN 9798874505899 (library binding) | ISBN 9798874505905 (paperback) | ISBN 9798874505912 (ebook other) | ISBN 9798874505936 (ebook other)
Subjects: LCSH: Salsa (Music)--History and criticism--Juvenile literature.
Classification: LCC ML3535.5 .W55 2025 (print) | LCC ML3535.5 (ebook) | DDC 781.64--dc23/eng/20241015
LC record available at https://lccn.loc.gov/2024048584
LC ebook record available at https://lccn.loc.gov/2024048585

Printed in Guangzhou, China
1 2 3 4 5 6 7 8 9 0 29 28 27 26 25

042025
100924

Art Director: Terry Paulhus **Project Coordinator:** Heather Kissock